Essential Lives

BARACK OBAMA

WITHDRAWN

BARACK

OBAMA

44TH U.S. PRESIDENT

by **Tom Robinson**

Content Consultant:
Wilbur C. Rich, PhD
William R. Kenan, Jr. Professor of Political Science
Department of Political Science, Wellesley College

ABDO
Publishing Company

CREDITS

Published by ABDO Publishing Company, 8000 West 78th Street, Edina, Minnesota 55439. Copyright © 2009 by Abdo Consulting Group, Inc. International copyrights reserved in all countries. No part of this book may be reproduced in any form without written permission from the publisher. The Essential Library™ is a trademark and logo of ABDO Publishing Company.

Printed in the United States.

Editor: Melissa Johnson
Copy Editor: Paula Lewis
Interior Design and Production: Nicole Brecke
Cover Design: Becky Daum

Library of Congress Cataloging-in-Publication Data
Robinson, Tom, 1964-
    Barack Obama : 44th U.S. president / by Tom Robinson.
        p. cm. — (Essential lives)
    Includes bibliographical references and index.
    ISBN 978-1-60453-527-3
    1. Obama, Barack—Juvenile literature. 2. Presidents—United States—Biography—Juvenile literature. 3. Legislators—United States—Biography—Juvenile literature. 4. African American legislators—Biography—Juvenile literature. 5. United States. Congress. Senate—Biography—Juvenile literature. 6. Racially mixed people—United States—Biography—Juvenile literature. I. Title.

E901.1.O23R63 2009
973.931092—dc22
[B]
                                        2008047741

TABLE OF CONTENTS

Barack Obama, the forty-fourth president of the United States

THE NEW PRESIDENT

More than 125,000 people gathered in Grant Park in Chicago, Illinois, on the night of November 4, 2008. The crowd had come hoping to witness history. Within hours, the results of the 2008 presidential election would be in. If the

Democratic candidate Barack Obama won, he would become the first African-American president of the United States.

The nation watched as the polls closed and the votes were counted state by state. Early in the evening, the major news networks declared that Obama, a senator from Illinois, had won Pennsylvania. With that win, it became unlikely that Obama's opponent, Arizona senator John McCain, would win. Soon, most of the Great Lakes states and New England had declared for Obama. After the polls closed in California, Oregon, and Washington at 11:00 p.m. Eastern Standard Time, Obama had collected more than the 270 Electoral College votes needed to win. The people of the United States had elected Barack Obama as their forty-fourth president.

The crowd at Grant Park went wild as the news networks made

The Electoral College

In the United States, the president is not simply the person who receives the most votes, which is known as the popular vote. Instead, the United States uses the Electoral College. In this system, each state has a specific number of electors, depending on the state's population. Whichever candidate gets the most votes in each state receives all the votes of that state's electors. The Electoral College has 538 total votes, and a candidate must receive 270 votes to win.

Usually, the candidate who wins the Electoral College also has won the popular vote. In 2008, President Barack Obama won about 52 percent of the popular vote. However, it is possible to win the Electoral College while losing the popular vote.

Supporters gathered in Chicago's Grant Park to witness Obama's presidential victory speech.

the announcement. Soon after McCain made his concession speech in Arizona, Obama took the stage in Chicago. He greeted the crowd and began his victory speech,

> *If there is anyone out there who still doubts that America is a place where all things are possible; who still wonders if the dream of our founders is alive in our time; who still questions the power of our democracy, tonight is your answer.*[1]

His words told of the hope and patriotism of the American people. He spoke of the difficulties the nation faced. He asked the people to join with him in working to remake the country. He recounted historic changes of the last century. Finally, he asked, "If our children should live to see the next century; if my daughters should be so lucky to live [so long], what change will they see? What progress will we have made?"[2] The president-elect challenged the people to move forward with him into the future.

A Historic Moment

Less than half a century earlier, race divided the United States. The bitter legacy of slavery still lingered, as African Americans were kept segregated by law or by habit in many places. Across the South, unfair laws prevented most African Americans from voting. African Americans and other members of the civil rights movement held sit-ins, boycotts, and demonstrations to secure equal rights for all Americans. Racial tensions erupted into riots and other forms of violence across the nation. On April 4, 1968, a great leader of

Books by Obama

Obama is the author or coauthor of several books, including:

- *Dreams from My Father: A Story of Race and Inheritance*
- *The Audacity of Hope: Thoughts on Reclaiming the American Dream*
- *It Takes a Nation: How Strangers Became Family in the Wake of Hurricane Katrina*
- *Change We Can Believe In: Barack Obama's Plan to Renew America's Promise*

the movement, Dr. Martin Luther King Jr., was assassinated in Memphis, Tennessee. King's greatest dream had been of a country united, where people of all races would be equal.

In the years since 1968, many of the country's racial problems improved. New laws protected the rights of African Americans and other minority groups. The dream of a post-racial America began to seem possible. African Americans, however, were still underrepresented in the government. Few minorities had reached high offices. While several African Americans served in the U.S. Congress, their numbers were never in proportion to the African-American population. Two African Americans had also become secretary of state, a close adviser to the president. But no minority had ever been president.

After Obama's election was announced, Congressman John Lewis spoke. Lewis had been a young leader of the civil rights movement with Dr. King. He recounted the struggles and suffering of those who had worked to make this historic moment possible. He noted that this victory was not just Obama's, but a triumph of the American people. He said, "We have witnessed tonight . . . a revolution of values, a revolution of ideals. There's been a transformation of America, and it will have unbelievable influence on the world."[3]

BEYOND RACE

Although Barack Obama was the first minority candidate of a major political party, and became the first minority president of the United States, he avoided making the campaign about race. As the child of a white mother and an African father, Obama had a unique perspective on the nation's racial problems. He made it clear

African-American Presidential Candidates

Shirley Chisholm became the first African-American woman to serve in Congress when she was elected to the U.S. House of Representatives in 1969. In 1972, she was also the first African American to run for president. She died in 2005 at the age of 80.

The Reverend Jesse Jackson ran for the Democratic nomination in 1984 and 1988. Jackson is a prominent civil rights activist and the founder of the Rainbow Coalition.

Lenora Fulani, a self-described radical activist, ran as an independent candidate in 1988. She became the first African American and first woman to be on the presidential ballot in all 50 states.

Alan Keyes is a former Assistant Secretary of State for International Organizations under President Ronald Reagan. He ran for the Republican nomination in 1996, 2000, and 2008. Keyes also ran against and lost to Barack Obama in the 2004 U.S. Senate race in Illinois.

The Reverend Al Sharpton ran for the Democratic nomination in 2004. Sharpton is a civil rights and social justice activist.

Carol Moseley Braun was the first African-American woman to become a U.S. senator. In 2004, she was the only woman to pursue the Democratic nomination for president.

that he wanted to build bridges between the races and solve the country's problems as a united group.

Obama had a history of transcending race. As a law student at Harvard University, Obama led the student law journal—the first African-American student to do so. Working with conservatives and liberals, he led the journal through a number of difficult racial issues. As a candidate for the U.S. Senate in 2004, Obama gave the speech that made him famous at the 2004 Democratic National Convention. He spoke of his hope that all Americans could unite in an effort to improve the country.

In March 2008, Obama spoke on the topic of race. He grieved that racism had pitted blacks and whites against each other and that the legacy of discrimination still harmed the African-American community. He acknowledged that the complex issue of race could not be ignored. However, he stressed his belief that whites and blacks could work together to heal the wounds of racism.

> *But what we know—what we have seen—is that America can change. That is the true genius of this nation. What we have already achieved gives us hope—the audacity to hope—for what we can and must achieve tomorrow.*[4]

President-elect Barack Obama and vice president-elect Joe Biden
took the stage on election night, November 4, 2008.

Nine-year-old Barack with his stepfather, mother, and baby sister

A Boy Named Barry

Barack Obama's parents were an unlikely couple. Barack Obama Sr. was born and raised in Kenya. His intelligence helped him win a college scholarship. He became the first African student at the University of Hawaii. Ann Dunham was a white woman who grew up in Kansas. She lived in Oklahoma, California, Texas, and Washington before moving to Honolulu, Hawaii, with her parents and entering the university.

Barack Obama Sr. and Ann Dunham met in a Russian class in 1960. They married on February 2, 1961, when Ann was three months pregnant. They told no one until after the wedding. At that time, interracial marriage was uncommon—in some states, it was even illegal. Barack Sr. already had a wife and two children in Kenya. Having more than one wife was legal in Kenya. However, Barack Sr.'s family opposed his marriage to a white woman from the United States. Ann's parents were upset at first, but they supported their daughter's decision. Barack Hussein Obama Jr. was born on August 4, 1961.

Barack Sr. left to pursue his doctorate degree at Harvard University in Massachusetts in 1963. Ann and their two-year-old son stayed behind in Hawaii. While at Harvard, Barack Sr. did not return to Hawaii to visit the family.

Barack's Mother

Barack's mother was called "Ann," but her name was actually Stanley Ann Dunham. Ann's father wanted a boy and gave his daughter his first name when she was born.

Later in life, Ann earned her PhD in anthropology. She started small loan programs to help the women of Indonesia. Ann, who was born on November 29, 1942, died of cancer on November 7, 1995.

Also, Barack Sr. planned to return to Kenya when he completed his education. Ann did not want to follow him to Africa, so the two divorced in 1964. Barack Sr. later became an economist in the Kenyan government.

GRANDPARENTS

Barack's grandfather, Stan Dunham, was a World War II veteran and a furniture salesman. He moved his family around a lot, until they finally settled in Hawaii. His wife, Madelyn, worked to help support the family. She eventually rose through the ranks to become one of the first female vice presidents of the Bank of Hawaii.

Ann continued her studies at the University of Hawaii after her divorce. She and her son moved in with her parents. They helped care for Barack, who was called "Barry" as a little boy. But money was tight in the shared household—at one point, Ann used food stamps to feed her son. Barack's grandparents were a very important part of his childhood. They often took the role of parents while Barack's father, and sometimes mother, were away. Barack learned to rely on "Gramps" and "Toot," which is the Hawaiian word for "grandma."

Barack was close to his grandparents, who helped raise him.

LIVING IN INDONESIA

After Barack's father left, Ann completed her degree in anthropology at the University of Hawaii. While there, she met and married Lolo Soetoro in 1967. Soetoro, an Indonesian, soon brought his new family home with him to Jakarta, the capital of Indonesia.

Barack attended schools in Jakarta, learning the Indonesian language. His first school was a Catholic elementary school in an area traditionally controlled

Indonesia

Indonesia, where Barack began school, is a nation of about 17,000 islands. It is situated between the Indian and Pacific oceans in Southeast Asia. Many of its islands feature rain forests. The country is the fourth most populous in the world, with more than 22 million residents. Split over the many islands, residents speak 580 different languages and dialects. The majority of Indonesians are Muslim. The country's economy is built around oil and natural gas, and it is part of the Organization of Petroleum Exporting Countries (OPEC). Indonesia gained its independence from the Netherlands in 1949.

by Muslims. The school was a target for some neighborhood children, who sometimes threw rocks at it. Ann worried that the local schools were not academically challenging enough. Unable to afford to send Barack to the elite international school, Ann gave her son extra lessons every morning at 4:00 a.m.

After six months in Indonesia, six-year-old Barack was becoming comfortable with the country's language and traditions. He would later write in *Dreams from My Father,*

> *The children of farmers, servants, and low-level bureaucrats had become my best friends, and together we ran the streets morning and night, hustling odd jobs, catching crickets.* [1]

Barack learned the adventure of eating raw peppers, snake meat, and roasted grasshoppers, and looked forward to packages of chocolate and peanut butter from his grandparents in Hawaii. Soetoro also taught Barack boxing skills to help him defend himself, if necessary.

During this time, Barack used his stepfather's last name and was known as "Barry Soetoro." The family eventually moved to a nicer section of Jakarta after Soetoro took a better job with a U.S. oil company. During his last year in the country, Barack attended fourth grade in a public elementary school that was predominantly Muslim. Barack's half sister, Maya Soetoro-Ng, was born in Indonesia in 1970.

BACK TO HAWAII

In 1971, Ann sent ten-year-old Barack back to Hawaii to live with his grandparents. The Dunhams had helped Barack get a scholarship at the prestigious Punahou prep school. Barack's mother and sister returned to Hawaii later in the year, after Ann separated from Soetoro,

Fitting In

In his memoir, *Dreams from My Father*, Obama wrote of some of the troubles he had while growing up. Obama remembered returning to Hawaii to live with his grandparents. Excited to see each other at first, the conversation turned to an uncomfortable silence as the young boy realized he hardly knew these people he had come to live with.

He wrote of his disappointment starting school in Hawaii. Young Barack was excited to attend Punahou School, until he arrived on the first day. He was different from the other students, because of his African father and his childhood in Indonesia. The other children teased him and he had trouble making friends.

Barack's stepfather. Barack's father, Barack Sr., who wanted to visit while he recovered from an accident, contacted the family in Hawaii. Barack got to know his long-lost father during the extended visit. This was the last time he saw his father, who died in a 1982 car accident.

Ann returned to Indonesia in 1976, but Barack, who was preparing for his sophomore year at Punahou School, decided to stay in Hawaii and live with his grandparents. Maya Soetoro-Ng, Obama's younger sister, explained,

Father's Visit

Barack saw his father for the last time during Barack Sr.'s stay in Hawaii in 1971. In *Dreams from My Father*, Obama wrote that he did not remember many of the specific events of the month he shared with his father. Instead, he could recall a series of images, such as posing for pictures in front of the Christmas tree, or feeling his father's hand on his shoulder as Barack Sr. introduced him to old college friends.

Young Barack was nervous when Barack Sr. wanted to visit his school. The other students had teased him about his African father. But, after Barack Sr. visited Barack's fifth grade class, the other students were impressed with his stories of life in Kenya. Barack was thrilled with his classmates' reactions, and his admiration for his father grew.

Barack Sr. and Barack's grandparents, however, did not agree on the best way to raise Barack. A conflict arose when Barack Sr. noticed Barack viewing *How the Grinch Stole Christmas*. He complained that Barack watched too much television and should be studying. Having made the commitment to raising Barack, his grandparents were offended at the criticism. They knew Barack looked forward to watching the once-a-year Christmas cartoon. The adults shouted at each other, and the tension lasted for the rest of the visit.

I don't imagine the decision to let him stay behind was an easy one for anyone. But he wanted to remain at Punahou. He had friends there. He was comfortable there, and to a kid his age, that's all that mattered.[2]

Gramps and Toot's home became the common gathering place for Barack and many of his friends. Barack had an intellectual side and loved books. His friends remember discussing philosophy and world politics in Obama's bedroom after basketball practice.

Although his grandparents provided a loving home, Barack was not always happy and struggled with his identity. He focused less on his books and more on his basketball skills. In his memoir, Obama wrote about the adolescent problems he had growing up and defining himself as a black man.

In 1979, Barack graduated with honors from Punahou School. Although his mother and sister came from Indonesia to see him on that special day, Barack thanked his grandparents on his yearbook

Famous Relations

Obama's family tree extends deep into the past in North America and in Africa. Four hundred years ago, an ancestor on his father's side was a warrior and leader of the Luo tribe in Africa. In the United States, Obama has ancestors who fought in the Revolutionary War. He has ancestors who owned slaves and ancestors who fought for the North in the American Civil War. Obama and President Harry S. Truman are distantly related cousins. Obama also shares distant ancestors with President George W. Bush and Vice President Dick Cheney.

State Champs

Barack was known as "Barry O'Bomber" by his high school basketball teammates for his ability to hit long jump shots. Barack was one of the substitutes on the Punahou School basketball team that won a Hawaii state high school championship in 1978–1979, his senior year.

Barack retained his love of basketball after high school. Friends from Harvard remember his competitiveness in pickup games. For years, visits back to Hawaii included pickup games with old teammates.

In 2008, Obama made basketball a part of his presidential campaign. He played a 3-on-3 game as part of a voter registration drive in Indiana before the presidential primary.

page. At his wedding years later, Barack brought many people to tears when he spoke about his grandparents and how Toot made sure he never felt alone as a little boy.

In 2008, Toot grew very ill. The weekend before the presidential election, Barack stopped campaigning to visit her in Hawaii. It was the last time he ever saw her. She died on November 3, the day before the election. Although she did not live to see her grandson become president, she cast an absentee ballot before she died so she was able to vote for him.

Barack has always loved basketball. He played on the varsity squad during high school and plays pickup games to this day.

Obama studied political science at Columbia University in New York City.

COLLEGE AND COMMUNITY

Obama was able to choose between several colleges when he graduated from Punahou School. His choice was Occidental College in Los Angeles, California. Obama entered the college in 1979 on a full scholarship. Obama has happy memories of his time there. He explained in a 2007 interview,

> It's a wonderful, small liberal arts college. The professors were diverse and inspiring. I ended up making some lifelong friendships there, and those first two years really helped me grow up.[1]

During his freshman and sophomore years, Obama made his first conscious effort to become involved in political issues. Eric Newhall, a professor at Occidental, said Obama had a strong presence about him. Obama displayed a knack for writing and began developing his speaking abilities. "He came off as a serious, articulate, intelligent young guy," Newhall said.[2] Other professors remember Obama as thoughtful and curious.

Former classmate John Boyer has memories of driving around Los Angeles with Obama and sharing pizzas. Even in college, Obama

Occidental College

Occidental College was founded in 1887. It is a small liberal arts institution. It bills itself as a highly selective and diverse college in a big city. The school is located in the Eagle Rock section of Los Angeles, northeast of the city's downtown area.

Jack Kemp, a 1957 graduate of Occidental, was a Republican presidential candidate in 1988. The former National Football League quarterback was also a vice presidential candidate in 1996.

was able to communicate with those who had opposing views. Although Boyer describes himself as conservative, he said, "What I admired about him then and now is that he is a very principled person in how he formulated his views."[3]

Seeking Community

As a young man who lived in Indonesia and Hawaii and had roots in Kansas and Kenya, Obama was still looking for a place where he felt comfortable during his college years. Although of mixed race, he viewed himself as a black American. "What I needed was a community," Obama wrote in *Dreams from My Father*, ". . . a community that cut deeper than the common despair that black friends and I shared when reading the latest crime statistics, or the high fives I might exchange on a basketball court."[4]

The Eagle Rock section of Los Angeles, where Occidental is located, did not have the feel of true city living for Obama. When he heard of a transfer program with Columbia University, he decided to apply and moved to New York City. Obama wrote,

I figured that if there weren't any more black students at Columbia than there were at Oxy, I'd at least be in the heart of a true city, with black neighborhoods in close proximity. As it were, there wasn't much in L.A. to hold me back.[5]

MAKING A CHANGE

After two years at Occidental, Obama transferred to Columbia University during the summer of 1981. He made his decision in part because he wanted to attend a larger school. He also wanted the experience of studying in New York City. Obama, already a successful student, promised himself that he would be more serious about his studies and avoid potential trouble.

Attending Columbia while living in tiny off-campus apartments exposed Obama to some of the harsh realities of New York City. He saw extremes of poverty and enormous wealth in close proximity to each other. Obama had some involvement in the Black Students Organization and participated in anti-apartheid activities.

Most of Obama's time at Columbia, however, was spent concentrating on his studies. "When I transferred, I decided to buckle down and get serious," he said. "I spent a lot of time in the library. I didn't socialize that much. I was like a monk."[6] Obama graduated from Columbia in the spring of 1983. He received a Bachelor of Arts degree in political science with a concentration in international relations.

Columbia University

Columbia University is older than the United States. It was founded in 1754 as King's College by royal charter of King George II of England. It is the fifth-oldest university in the United States and the oldest in New York state. Based in Manhattan in New York City, the school was renamed Columbia University in 1784.

Jerry Kellman hired Obama to work as a community organizer in Chicago.

Taking a Break

After graduating from Columbia, Obama set
aside thoughts of attending law school or working in
the corporate world. "I always felt that the value of
a really good education is you can take more risks,"
Obama said in a 2004 interview. "Ultimately, if
I really need a job, if I've got to pay the bills, I'm
going to be able to find one."[7] Obama wanted to
work as a community organizer but could not find
the position he was seeking. Instead, he worked at
Business International Corporation as a research

analyst and then a financial writer. Many people would have considered this a successful start to a career. He left, however, to pursue his original goal of being an activist. Obama began working for the New York Public Interest and Research Group (NYPIRG), a nonprofit environmental group that focuses on the importance of recycling.

COMMUNITY ORGANIZER

In 1985, he was offered the position he was looking for with a nonprofit group in Chicago, Illinois. Jerry Kellman hired Obama to be a community organizer in Chicago for $10,000 a year. The offer included $2,000 for relocating, which the 23-year-old Obama used to buy an old car so he could make the move.

Once Obama arrived in Chicago, he worked to improve living conditions in poor neighborhoods with crime and high unemployment.

A Tiring Job

Jerry Kellman hired and supervised Barack Obama in his first community service job in Chicago. After watching Obama's dedication to long hours and his commitment to trying to make a difference, Kellman advised Obama to take more time off. As Kellman explained, Obama needed to build a personal life as well. Without outside support, an organizer could lose perspective and quickly burn out.

"I didn't heed [the] advice, though, perhaps because, as the bonds between myself and the leadership grew stronger, I found them offering more than simple friendship," said Obama.[8] He grew attached to the people in the community who were fighting for important causes.

He worked in the Roseland section of Chicago and helped the people of the Altgeld Gardens public housing development in the city's South Side.

In Altgeld, Obama worked with local churches to organize job training and other programs to help the poor and the working class. Obama said that the work helped him realize the importance of listening to people rather than following a predetermined agenda. "It was in these neighborhoods that I received the best education I ever had," he said.[9]

Kellman remembers Obama as eloquent and idealistic. Inspired by Dr. Martin Luther King Jr. and the civil rights movement of the 1950s and 1960s, Obama settled into his work with the Developing Communities Project (DCP). Obama fought battles large and small, such as coaxing the city to fill potholes or making sure apartment managers

A Believer

Linda Randle, a resident of the Altgeld Gardens public housing complex, worked with Obama in a frustrating battle with Chicago city officials. They were fighting to have asbestos, an insulating material that can cause cancer, removed from apartments.

Twenty years after working with Obama, Randle was still a resident of the complex. She believed Obama would be an effective president. "He has a great understanding of people," she said, "and he knows how to bring about change through compromise. That's what we need in Washington."[10]

made needed repairs. Working out of an office in the Holy Rosary Church, Obama learned the value of lengthy one-on-one conversations with neighborhood residents. These conversations helped him understand individual concerns and get a feel for what the community as a whole needed. That caring approach also helped when he organized the community to work together for a cause.

One of Obama's challenges included the church communities in African-American neighborhoods. The people he sought to help were often loyal to their churches, which were primarily Christian. They were unsure about the DCP, which was run by three white men—two of them Jewish. Obama had to overcome some people's biased distrust of the men he worked for.

Obama tried to convince the church leaders that he could help each of them specifically while he worked at the same time to help the larger community. The Reverend Alvin Love, a Baptist minister on the South Side of Chicago, recalls one such message from Obama: "There ought to be some way for us to help you meet your self-interest while at the same time meeting the real interests and the needs of the community."[11]

Obama made some progress in his community work. He felt, however, that he could make more significant changes if he could find a different way to solve problems. He decided to seek a law degree and enrolled at Harvard Law School in 1988.

Obama was a community organizer in Chicago
before and after he studied at Harvard.

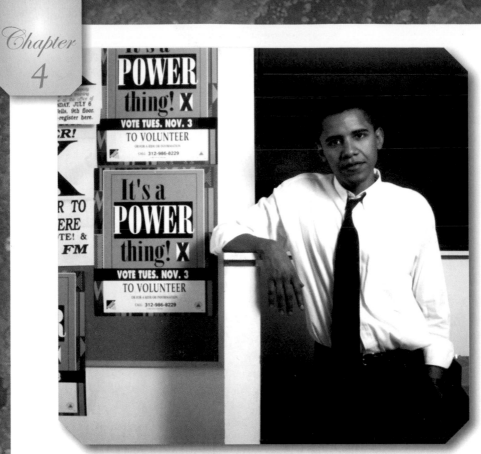

After graduating from Harvard Law School, Obama organized a successful voter registration drive in Chicago.

THE LAWYER

In 1987, Obama was still a community organizer in Chicago when his half sister Auma visited him. A daughter of Barack Sr. from his first marriage, she had never met her half brother before. She told Obama some things that he had not known about his father. These conversations seem to have been part of the reason that Obama soon decided to return to school. Obama's boss in Chicago, Jerry Kellman, spoke of a conversation the two men shared. Obama told Kellman that he was thinking about going back to school and starting a life in politics. Obama explained how his own father had become a beaten man because he could not pursue his ideals.

HIS FATHER'S MISTAKES

In *Dreams from My Father*, Obama wrote about two images of his father. The idolized view of a mystery man contrasted with the sad stories Auma told about their father's last years. Obama wrote,

> *All my life, I had carried a single image of my father, one that I sometimes rebelled against but had never questioned, one that I had later tried to take as my own. The brilliant scholar, the generous friend, the upstanding leader—my father had been all of those things.*[1]

Auma shared other stories of their father's life. After holding prominent political positions in Kenya, he had been dropped to lower-level positions during power struggles between the country's two

Barack Obama Sr. worked for the Kenyan government after he left the United States.

most powerful tribes. A bitter man who began to drink too much, Barack Sr. eventually lost his job. He may have been driving drunk at the time of the accident that took his life in 1982.

"That [idealized] image had suddenly vanished," Obama wrote. "Replaced by . . . what? A bitter drunk? An abusive husband? A defeated, lonely bureaucrat?"[2] Although he had once been inspired to live up to his father, Obama was now determined to avoid the mistakes that had defeated his father.

HARVARD AND MICHELLE

After three years of struggling to make changes on Chicago's South Side, Obama was accepted into Harvard Law School in 1988. Obama's professors were impressed by his ability to take complicated legal arguments and apply them to real-life social problems. Other students appreciated his diplomacy and his ability to help them clarify their own arguments.

After his first year at Harvard, Obama spent the summer of 1989 at the Chicago law firm of Sidley & Austin. During the summer, he met Michelle Robinson, a 1988 Harvard Law School graduate from Chicago. Michelle was his mentor at the firm. At first, she wanted to keep their relationship professional, but Obama kept asking her out. The young law

"For every one of me, there are thousands of young black kids with the same energies, enthusiasm and talent that I have who have not gotten the opportunity because of crime, drugs, and poverty. I think my election does symbolize progress but I don't want people to forget that there is still a lot of work to be done."[3]
—*Barack Obama, on becoming president of the* Harvard Law Review

student charmed her and she finally accepted.

Michelle Robinson grew up on the South Side of Chicago. Her mother, Marian Robinson, stayed home to raise Michelle and Michelle's older brother, Craig. Fraser Robinson, Michelle's father, worked for the Chicago water department. He battled multiple sclerosis and died less than one year before his daughter's marriage.

Michelle attended public school in Chicago and graduated from Princeton University and Harvard Law School. She returned to Chicago in 1988 to join the law firm of Sidley & Austin. Michelle decided after a few years at the law firm that she did not want to practice corporate law anymore. Having received an elite education, she believed that it was her duty to give back to her community instead, a belief she shares with Obama. Since that time, her jobs

Michelle's Jobs

Michelle has worked as assistant commissioner of planning and development for the city of Chicago. She helped found the Chicago chapter of Public Allies, an AmeriCorps program that prepares young people for public service. Michelle also worked for the University of Chicago in a variety of roles, beginning in 1996.

have all included a strong public service component.

HARVARD LAW REVIEW

After his summer at Sidley & Austin, Obama returned to Harvard with a more serious outlook on life. During his second year, he became the first African-American president of the *Harvard Law Review*, a legal journal run by students. The organization is technically independent from Harvard Law School. Students choose what will be published and run the review with the help of three staff members.

The *Harvard Law Review* acts as an academic forum and a research tool for professional business staff, practicing lawyers, and students. It is also a way for students to develop their editing and writing skills. Although students produce the *Review*, it is a highly respected resource within the legal community. Articles

Keynote Speaker

Barack Obama's speaking ability has been recognized since his days at Harvard. The Black Law Students Association usually invites an important professor or judge to give the keynote address at its annual conference. When Obama graduated in 1991, they went against tradition and asked Obama to speak.

Harvard law professor Randall L. Kennedy considered Obama's speech a call to action. Kennedy summarized, "We've gotten this education, we've gotten this great halo, this great career-enhancing benefit. Let's not just feather our nests. Let's go forward and address the many ills that confront our society."[4]

are written by professors, judges, and practitioners, but edited by the students.

Obama became the *Harvard Law Review* president when the conservative faction decided to support him after its own candidates had been eliminated. The conservatives felt that Obama would treat them fairly, even if he did not agree with them politically.

Civil Rights Connection

Obama had shown an early commitment to civil rights and improving society with his work as a community organizer after college. After graduating from Harvard Law School, Obama took a position with the law firm Miner, Barnhill & Galland. The firm is nationally known for its civil rights work and its commitment to community development and social justice issues.

As a professor at the University of Chicago Law School, Obama taught the next generation of lawyers to care about these same issues. One of the courses Obama taught at the University of Chicago was titled "Current Issues in Racism and the Law." The class took on a wide variety of issues, drawing information and opinions from Supreme Court decisions and historical documents. These included the writings of Dr. Martin Luther King Jr. and Malcolm X. Some of the controversies discussed included immigration policy, welfare, affirmative action, and public school financing.

Later, as a state senator in Illinois, Obama helped pass a law against racial profiling. He also helped reform the rules for interrogating murder suspects.

Race at Harvard

Racial issues caused a great deal of tension at Harvard. Obama had to keep debates among the members from getting in the way of their work. If Obama led the *Harvard Law Review* into too many racial issues, he would be caught in the middle of a divided staff. If he failed to be involved enough, he would alienate African-American and liberal students who counted on his leadership.

Obama respectfully listened to both sides of the arguments and convinced each that they were being heard. "He was leading the discussion but he wasn't trying to impose his own perspective on it," said classmate Thomas Perrelli, a former counsel to Attorney General Janet Reno. "He was much more mediating."[5]

Although the position was unpaid, Obama often spent 50 to 60 hours on his duties each week. Sometimes, he had to choose between his classes and the *Harvard Law Review*. Still, he managed to keep up his grades.

Winning the *Harvard Law Review* presidency led to new attention from the media. Obama signed a contract to write a book about his experiences with race in the United States. The book evolved into his memoir, *Dreams from My Father*, published in 1995.

Graduate

Obama graduated magna cum laude from Harvard Law School in 1991 and returned to

Chicago. He worked as a civil rights lawyer and
taught night classes at the University of Chicago Law
School.

As an honors graduate and former president
of the *Harvard Law Review,* Obama could have worked
almost anywhere. Instead, he wanted to go back
to helping people. He also wanted to stay close to
Michelle Robinson. Obama's media adviser and
friend, David Axelrod, was impressed by Obama's
commitment to noble work. "He could have written
his ticket anywhere and made a fortune in industry
or at a law firm," Axelrod said.[6]

Obama and Robinson were engaged when he
returned to work in Chicago. They were married on
October 3, 1992.

In 1992, Obama helped voter registration drives
in support of Bill Clinton's successful presidential
campaign. This work built on his pre-Harvard
community organizer experience. The strong push
to register voters, most of them African Americans,
also helped Democrat Carol Moseley Braun become
the first African-American woman elected to the
U.S. Senate.

In 1993, Obama joined the firm of Miner,
Barnhill & Galland. Obama was able to work on

Obama was a popular lecturer at the University of Chicago Law School.

causes that were important to him. He won cases involving voting rights and discrimination in employment and housing.

Teaching Law

After receiving his law degree, Obama also became a teacher. He spent ten years lecturing part-time at the University of Chicago Law School while continuing to work for the law firm during the day. Students there rated Obama as one of their top instructors. The response to his teaching style was so positive that the school wanted him to become a full-time teacher.

A budding political career prevented Obama from becoming a full-time educator. Obama said he loved teaching, but he wanted to pursue the opportunity to run for U.S. Senate. "I think some of the public speaking skills I developed in the classroom—stay on your toes; don't make answers too long—I'm using on the campaign trail."[7] Students praised Obama for a conversational style that made them feel that their viewpoints were being taken seriously.

Barack Obama and Michelle Robinson were married in 1992.

Obama sponsored key legislation in the Illinois Senate.

ENTERING POLITICS

With his history working as a community advocate, Obama was a natural choice to step forward when a new political position became open. Mel Reynolds was a Democrat and a member of the U.S. House of Representatives from the Second District in Illinois. When Reynolds was arrested in the summer of 1994, people began to speculate about who would fill his position.

Alice Palmer, an African-American community activist, decided to oppose Reynolds for his seat. At the time, Palmer represented Chicago's South Side, the Thirteenth District, in the Illinois Senate. Palmer announced that she would be giving up her state senate seat. She also recommended Obama as the Democratic candidate to fill her vacated position. The district included the University of Chicago and Obama's recently purchased home.

Obama began the process of campaigning for Palmer's open state senate seat in July 1995. He announced plans to run and filed papers to create a fund-raising committee in August. He officially declared himself a candidate for the Illinois Senate in September.

CIRCUMSTANCES CHANGE

Reynolds was convicted in September and announced that he would resign from the U.S. House of Representatives, effective October 1, 1995. With a year left on Reynolds's term, a special election was announced for November 28, 1995, so

Chicago Politics

Chicago is known for its history of "machine" politics. A political machine runs on a system of patronage, where the governing party grants favors and jobs in return for votes. Although the worst of the corruption in Chicago has ended, politics in the city are still cutthroat. Dealing with the city's politics helped Obama prepare for almost anything he might face in national politics.

"I don't think he would have ended up where he is if he hadn't come to Chicago," said Jerry Kellman, who first hired Obama as a community organizer. "It's where he got an incredible education in real politics."[1] Kellman said battling Chicago politics helped turn Obama's idealism into a more realistic and practical approach.

that voters could select Reynolds's replacement. Palmer was soundly beaten by Jesse Jackson Jr., the son of the civil rights leader and former presidential candidate. She finished third behind Emil Jones Jr.

With the encouragement of many people, Palmer decided to run for her state senate seat after all. Her decision threw Chicago politics into confusion. Some influential Chicago Democrats wanted Obama to stop campaigning and avoid challenging Palmer. Others felt that Palmer had made her decision when she ran for the U.S. House of Representatives office. They believed that Palmer should step aside.

Obama had a working campaign staff and was not ready to give up. He risked alienating powerful Democrats. If he lost to Palmer, he could damage his future in politics. The choice was not an easy one, but he decided to proceed.

As a state senator, Obama worked in the Illinois State Capitol in Springfield.

Before starting a campaign, Obama had suggested that Palmer keep her options open and file for both positions in case the congressional attempt did not go well. Palmer declined and encouraged Obama to move forward. "I certainly did say that I wasn't going to run," Palmer said. "There's no question about that."[2]

Obama said it would be difficult to step down after raising money, hiring staff, and making other commitments, such as opening a campaign office. "I liked Alice Palmer a lot," he said. "I thought she was a good public servant. It was very awkward. That part of it I wish had played out entirely differently."[3]

Palmer was days away from a December 18 deadline to file a nominating petition to make her eligible to run. She needed at least 757 signatures from district voters. She met the deadline and submitted 1,580 signatures.

CHALLENGING THE PETITIONS

Ballot challenges are legal in Chicago and a frequent part of the city's politics. On January 2, 1996, the Obama campaign filed protests with the Chicago Board of Election Commissioners. These protests challenged hundreds of signatures on the nominating petitions of Palmer and three other candidates. When the challenges were over, only Obama was left in the race. Palmer dropped out, and the commissioners found the other candidates ineligible.

Ronald Davis, a consultant paid by the Obama campaign, organized the review of the petitions. He said Obama wondered how it would look to knock everyone off the ballot. Eventually, however, Obama decided to allow Davis to file the objections.

Gha-is Askia, one of the candidates eliminated that day, wondered if Obama was being honorable by not letting the people decide among a larger group of candidates. Palmer supporter Timuel Black, on the other hand, said that any other politician also would have challenged the petitions. Obama was troubled by the decision to challenge the nominations, but he said it was important for everyone to follow the rules. Moreover, as Obama explained later, he worried that "if you couldn't run a successful petition drive, then that raised questions in terms of how effective a representative you were going to be."[4]

With the strong Democratic hold on the district, Obama's work was essentially over. He faced no serious challenge in the general election and won easily.

Updating the List

Chicago officials completed a routine update of the Thirteenth District voting list in 1995. This update took the names of 15,871 people off the list of registered voters.

Some rivals of Barack Obama had relied on old polling records from earlier in 1995 to check the signatures of registered voters. In the challenge, Obama's people used the newest list of voters. Records show that some of the successful challenges were a result of the differences between the two lists.

State Senator

Obama served as an Illinois state senator for eight years. He focused his early political career on helping families and continuing the community service work he did before entering politics. He helped working families through programs such as the state Earned Income Tax Credit, which gave $100 million in tax cuts to families across the state. He also fought for more early childhood education and helped negotiate welfare reform.

After a number of death row inmates were found innocent, Obama worked with law enforcement to change interrogation rules for murder cases. The police would now have to videotape interrogations and confessions in these cases. He also helped pass a law against racial profiling.

Arguably, Obama's most important legislation in the Illinois

Hyde Park

Obama began his political career from the Hyde Park neighborhood on Chicago's South Side. Hyde Park is an upscale community surrounded by poorer areas. Compared to some parts of Chicago, Hyde Park is relatively integrated, with white and black families living side by side. The University of Chicago is in the center of Hyde Park. Poorer, mostly African-American neighborhoods ring the edges of the area. Hyde Park is known for its liberal politics and also for standing up to the established Chicago political machine, which controlled city government for decades.

Senate was his work on campaign finance reform. Working on a small bipartisan committee, Obama helped make a compromise that the senate passed. Although Obama favored contribution limits, he knew that the senate would not vote for that.

Instead, the bill passed with reforms that stopped lobbyist gifts and banned legislators from spending campaign money on personal items. The new law also required campaigns to disclose their donors and post their reports electronically. Journalists used the new database to expose corruption, changing Illinois's political reporting.

Unsuccessful Attempt

Barack Obama misjudged how quickly he could climb through the ranks in politics when he challenged Bobby Rush for his U.S. House of Representatives seat in 2000. Rush was a formidable opponent. The former Black Panther member had already served four terms as a representative. His district included Obama's state senate district. At the time, Obama thought that Rush might be vulnerable because Rush had recently run for mayor but lost badly.

However, Rush comfortably won the primary with 61 percent of the votes to Obama's 30. Obama continued in the Illinois Senate for four more years before winning a seat in the U.S. Senate.

Political pollster Ron Lester said it was a case of challenging the wrong opponent in the wrong place. "Taking on Bobby Rush among black voters is like running into a buzz saw," Lester said.

His support ran deep—to the extent that a lot of people who liked Barack still wouldn't support him because they were committed to Bobby. [Rush] had built up this reserve of goodwill over 25 years in that community.[5]

Speaking of his time in the Illinois Senate, Obama said, "I learned that if you're willing to listen to people, it's possible to bridge a lot of the differences that dominate the national political debate."[6]

State Senator Emil Jones Jr., left, was one of Obama's political mentors.

Obama and wife Michelle with their daughters Malia, left, and Sasha

FAMILY LIFE

bama enjoyed many things about life on the campaign trail as a presidential candidate in 2008. He mentioned one glaring negative during an interview: "It's thrilling except I'm not seeing my wife and kids enough."[1] Barack and Michelle Obama have two daughters—Malia, born in 1998, and Sasha, born in 2001.

Obama's days sometimes seemed dull to his young daughters. He continued, "When I call them and they say, 'Daddy, what did you do today?' I said, 'Well, I spoke to 35,000 people.' It's like 'Boring.' It's not interesting [to them]."[2]

The Kids

Obama's interviews on the campaign trail covered a variety of subjects. They ranged from serious discussions of political issues to questions about what life was like in the Obama house. During the presidential campaign, the Obamas tried to keep Malia's and Sasha's lives as normal as possible. The girls continued piano lessons, played soccer, and got an allowance—one dollar a week—for doing chores. The Obamas kept their daughters

Barack Obama's Family

- Wife: Michelle Obama, formerly Michelle Robinson.
- Children: Two daughters, Malia and Sasha.
- Parents: Barack Obama Sr. and Ann Dunham, both deceased.
- Maternal grandparents: Stan and Madelyn Dunham, who raised Obama when his parents were out of the country. Both are deceased.
- Siblings: Barack has eight half siblings. Barack Obama Sr. had three sons, Abongo (Roy), Abo, and Bernard, and a daughter, Auma, with his first wife. Following his divorce from Ann Dunham, Barack Obama Sr. married again and had two more sons, David (deceased) and Mark. Barack Obama Sr. also has a son, George, from another relationship. Ann Dunham married again and had a daughter, Maya Soetoro-Ng.

away from the campaign most of the time so the girls would not get too used to being the center of attention.

Malia and Sasha had mixed feelings about the possibility of their father becoming president. The young girls worried that they would lose their Chicago friends if they moved to Washington DC. However, the girls were excited about the prospect of living in the White House. Malia especially looked forward to decorating her new room. In his presidential victory speech, Obama also promised the girls a new puppy when they moved.

THE GRANDMOTHER

The Obamas felt comfortable going out on the campaign trail because they could leave their daughters in good hands. Michelle's mother, Marian Robinson, lived only four miles (6 km) from the Obamas. She was able to watch the girls when

Tenth Birthday

Malia Obama had an exciting experience for her tenth birthday, which fell on July 4, 2008, in the middle of the presidential campaign. Malia joined her parents and her little sister, Sasha, in filming a television interview in Butte, Montana, with *Access Hollywood*. The girls were eager for the interview to end so they could go out for ice cream. They admitted that listening to their father's speeches could be boring for young girls and that they took water pistols along on the campaign trail to have some fun.

Michelle's mother, Marian Robinson

Michelle and Barack were away. Although Marian might have wanted to spoil her granddaughters, Michelle was a disciplinarian, so there were some disagreements between mother and grandmother. The two reached a compromise: when Marian came to the Obama house to watch the girls, Malia and Sasha ate organic food and were allowed only one hour of television. When the girls went to grandma's house, however, Marian treated her granddaughters to candy and later bedtimes.

WORK AND FAMILY

When Michelle Obama met with people on the campaign trail, one of her favorite topics was the need to balance work and family. She moved on from a law career to work in the University of Chicago administration as associate dean of student services and vice president of community and external affairs. Along with this work, she made her own contributions to community service. With her help, the University of Chicago Medical Center attracted four times as many volunteers than it had previously. Employees, in turn, volunteered for five times as many projects outside the hospital.

Michelle is focused on raising her daughters. Her life's work has centered around helping other families raise healthy children, values she brought with her to the White House. She says,

Role Models

Obama said that when his daughters need a role model they do not need to look far. "They know that no one is more together than their mom," Barack said of his wife, Michelle. He described Michelle as "very strong, tough, self-possessed . . . but she is also, I think, a person who feels very deeply."[5]

Obama's grandmother also provided a strong female example for his daughters. During World War II, Madelyn worked as an aircraft inspector while her husband was in the army. Later, Madelyn became a vice president of the Bank of Hawaii.

My first priority will always be to make sure that our girls are healthy and grounded. . . . Then, I want to help other families get the support they need, not just to survive, but to thrive. Policies that support families aren't political issues. They're personal. They're the causes I carry with me every single day.[3]

STAYING INVOLVED

The busy hours that are part of being a lawyer or a public servant can make balancing work and family difficult. Michelle always made sure to remind her husband of his responsibilities at home.

In *The Audacity of Hope*, Obama acknowledged that there were tense

The Challenge of Parenting

Barack Obama wrote about the challenges of parenting and working in *The Audacity of Hope*. He wrote about some difficult situations that happened before his daughters began school. He realized, however, that it must be much more difficult for other working parents. Because Barack and Michelle Obama both worked in professional jobs, they could rearrange their schedules when necessary. They could handle family emergencies without the risk of losing their jobs. The Obamas could also afford reliable child care, babysitters, and summer camps. If they needed help with their other household chores, they could get take-out dinners or pay someone to clean the house. Michelle's mother was also nearby to help.

Obama said it is necessary for the government to help the people who do not have those luxuries. "If we're serious about family values, then we can put policies in place that make the juggling of work and parenting a little bit easier," he wrote.[4]

times at home in their first year as parents. Michelle returned to work and his schedule intensified with the combination of legislative responsibilities and teaching college courses. The demands at home were not always equally split between the two working parents.

As a U.S. senator, Obama made sure to be home in Chicago Thursdays through Sundays whenever possible. Moving to the White House allowed the Obamas to eat dinner together again on a regular basis. —

Obama enjoyed a vacation with his family in Hawaii in August 2008.

Obama wrote his own keynote speech for the 2004 Democratic National Convention.

THE SPEECH

bama walked onto the stage at the Fleet Center in Boston, Massachusetts, a little after 9:00 p.m. on July 27, 2004. In the next 17 minutes, Obama would alter his future and potentially that of an entire nation. With his powerful delivery of the keynote speech at the 2004 Democratic National Convention, Obama burst onto the national political scene.

As Eli Saslow wrote in the *Washington Post* four years later:

> *Obama approached the lectern in Boston a virtual nobody, a representative of 600,000 constituents in Illinois' 13th District. He exited having set the course for an unprecedented political ascent, with the fortified self-confidence that he could deliver when it mattered most.*[1]

How Did He Get There?

Obama was an unlikely choice for the keynote address, which he acknowledged in the opening words of his speech. At the time, Obama was just a state senator running for the U.S. Senate. At his only previous national convention, just four years earlier, Obama could not even get to the convention floor.

Nominating Presidential Candidates

The presidential election occurs every four years. Prior to the election, there are a series of state primary elections. Delegates of the Democratic and Republican parties then gather at separate conventions to nominate their candidate for president of the United States.

For most of the nineteenth century, nominees needed to receive two-thirds of the votes from their party's delegates. This meant that additional rounds of voting would continue until one candidate prevailed in each party.

Today, most delegates are selected through state elections. Pledged delegates must vote for a certain candidate, based on the elections in their home state. Superdelegates, usually elected officials or heavily involved members of the Democratic Party, can vote for their preferred candidate and are often the reason one candidate wins over another.

An Outsider

In 2000, Obama, then a state senator from Illinois, made a late decision to attend the Democratic National Convention in Los Angeles. Obama hurried from Chicago to Los Angeles by plane. He was delayed at the airport when his credit card was declined as he tried to rent a car. Once the credit card and car rental issues were resolved, Obama could not get the credentials he needed to get to the convention floor. Obama was stuck watching speeches on a giant video screen outside the arena. He went home before the convention was over.

Obama, however, had a campaign staff as daring as he was. With his own campaign for the U.S. Senate going smoothly, Obama campaigned with John Kerry. As the Democratic nominee for president, Kerry had the power to select convention speakers. Jim Cauley, Obama's campaign manager for his U.S. Senate race, asked the Kerry campaign staff to include Obama at the convention.

Jack Corrigan, who organized the convention for Kerry, saw potential in the idea. Corrigan said,

> The hesitation on him as a speaker was that he didn't even hold federal office yet, so how prominent could he be? He was unproven. But we became convinced that he also offered incredible promise.[2]

The purpose of the convention was to formally complete the 2004 primary season and officially nominate Kerry as the Democrats' presidential candidate. One of the most memorable parts of the convention, however, was Obama's speech. It launched him onto the national stage and made his 2008 presidential candidacy possible.

GETTING READY

Obama was in Springfield, the capital of Illinois, performing his duties as a state senator when he learned that he had been selected to speak. He began work on his speech immediately.

Many politicians have speechwriters. Obama's higher-ranking staff members had sometimes handled the chore on complex political issues. One of Obama's skills as a politician, however, was his writing ability. He wanted the speech to be his own.

Obama worked on the speech in his hotel room at night. He wrote the first draft by hand on a yellow legal pad. "He wanted everything to be in his own words," Cauley said. "He guarded it. He made it clear from the beginning that this speech was going to be his baby."[3]

Obama produced a 25-minute speech. Convention officials suggested he cut it in half. Compromises were reached and Obama's

Obama helped Senator John Kerry campaign for president in 2004. Kerry invited Obama to speak at the Democratic National Convention.

staff helped him tighten the speech. Trimming unnecessary words resulted in the 17-minute speech he would deliver in Boston.

Obama was already an accomplished speaker, but he had never spoken while reading his notes from a teleprompter. Advisers rented a teleprompter so Obama could practice before the convention. Obama practiced the speech 15 times in his Chicago campaign offices. He practiced another three times after he arrived in Boston.

A nervous Obama knew that he had to give the perfect speech. He made special arrangements for his wife, Michelle, to join him backstage. She would help him keep calm in the moments before the biggest speech of his life.

MEMORABLE WORDS

Some critics debated how much substance Obama's speech had that night. Whatever the substance, no one can deny his impact. In those 17 minutes, he went from an unknown in national politics to a potential future president.

While telling Americans why they should vote for Kerry in 2004, at the same time he was showing many why they might vote for him one day. Mixed in with the frequent Kerry references were messages that made him attractive as a future candidate.

Obama started by pointing out just how unlikely his own arrival on the Fleet Center stage was. He told the story of his African father, a goat herder, and grandfather, a former domestic servant. He told about being the child of a black man from Kenya and a white woman from Kansas.

An Introduction

Obama's campaign staff was busy in the days before the 2004 Democratic National Convention in Boston. Among the biggest questions at the convention were "who is Barack Obama?" and "why is he the keynote speaker?" Obama spoke on television many times in the final days before his speech. Staff members passed out Obama signs on the floor of the convention center. Others passed out flyers for a postspeech party at a Boston nightclub.

Although the staff may have been afraid that no one would show up at the party, they should not have worried. After Obama's electrifying speech, people lined up around the block to enter the packed club.

Barack Obama then spoke about dreams of success:

My parents shared not only an improbable love; they shared an abiding faith in the possibilities of this nation. They would give me an African name, Barack, or "blessed," believing that in a tolerant America, your name is no barrier to success. They imagined me going to the best schools in the land, even though they weren't rich, because in a generous America, you don't have to be rich to achieve your potential.

He stressed the importance of diversity in America:

I stand here today grateful for the diversity of my heritage, aware that my parents' dreams live on in my two precious daughters. I stand here knowing that my story is part of the larger American story, that I owe a debt to all those who came before me, and that in no other country on Earth is my story even possible.

He spoke of the freedom that citizens of the United States enjoy:

> *We can say what we think, write what we think, without hearing a sudden knock on the door; that we can have an idea and start our own business without paying a bribe; [and] that we can participate in the political process without fear of retribution . . .*

He discussed the importance of personal responsibility:

> *People don't expect government to solve all their problems. But they sense, deep in their bones, that with a slight change in priorities, we can make sure that every child in America has a decent shot at life and that the doors of opportunity remain open to all. They know we can do better.*

He stressed the nation's obligation to people in the armed services:

> *When we send our young men and women into harm's way, we have a solemn obligation not to fudge the numbers or shade the truth about why they are going, to take care of their families while they're gone, to tend the soldiers upon their return and to never, ever go to war without enough troops to win the war, secure the peace, and earn the respect of the world.*

He spoke of the importance of helping one's community and those in need:

> If there's a child on the south side of Chicago who can't read, that matters to me, even if it's not my child. If there's a senior citizen somewhere who can't pay for their prescription and having to choose between medicine and the rent, that makes my life poorer even if it's not my grandparent. If there's an Arab-American family being rounded up without benefit of an attorney or due process, that threatens my civil liberties. It is that fundamental belief—I am my brother's keeper, I am my sister's keeper—that makes this country work.

He affirmed that despite many differences, Americans are very much the same. And he spoke of his belief in the nation, that the country will continue to improve in the future:

> Hope in the face of difficulty, hope in the face of uncertainty, the audacity of hope: In the end, that is God's greatest gift to us, the bedrock of this nation, a belief in things not seen, a belief that there are better days ahead. I believe that we can give our middle class relief and provide working families with a road to opportunity. I believe we can provide jobs for the jobless, homes for the homeless, and reclaim young people in cities across America from violence and despair.[4]

The Reaction

Obama walked off the stage and into a different life. His private life was gone. His time would be in constant demand. An entire country now seemed focused on Obama, assessing whether he should be a future leader. "That speech was his launch," said Dick Durbin, a U.S. senator from Illinois who introduced Obama that night. "It changed everything for him."[5]

Terry Link, a fellow Illinois state senator, watched the speech proudly as he recognized many of the lines. Obama had tested some of his ideas on Link in the days leading up to the convention. Link was moved to tears and soon realized he was not alone.

2004 Convention Highlights

The Democratic Party had its first extended look at its future leader, Barack Obama, during its 2004 national convention in Boston. There were, however, more immediate goals at the time of the convention. The convention formally made John Kerry the party's nominee to run against incumbent President George W. Bush.

Throughout the convention, various prominent party members spoke. They repeated the themes that they had hoped would help Kerry win in the November election. Party members consistently spoke about the issues of the election. They explained how the Democrats would be tough on terrorism and how it was necessary to make health care more affordable.

Pollsters and the media agreed that the 2004 convention energized Democrats and explained the party's ideas to the country. Obama's speech especially excited people across the country. Ultimately, despite a close election, President Bush won a second term.

"I turn around and I see there's not a dry eye in the whole place," Link said. "He got to *everybody*."[6]

Obama gave the keynote address at the Democratic National Convention on July 27, 2004. The speech launched him into the national spotlight.

Obama campaigned for U.S. Senate in the summer of 2004.

NATIONAL OFFICE

By the time of the 2004 election,
Obama was getting used to being in the
spotlight. He had already been the keynote speaker
at the Democratic National Convention. The speech
may have helped Illinois voters choose him to be

their U.S. senator. Obama received 70 percent of the votes and became the only African-American U.S. senator at the time. He became the fifth African-American U.S. senator and only the third since the Reconstruction Era after the American Civil War.

A CHANGING NATION

Obama had fallen short in an attempt to run for the U.S. House of Representatives in 2000. "It was an ill-considered race, and I lost badly—the sort of drubbing that awakens you to the fact that life is not obliged to work out as you'd planned," Obama wrote in *The Audacity of Hope*.[1]

More than a year later, after the terrorist attacks of September 11, 2001, Obama met with a media consultant who had been encouraging him to run for a higher office. The consultant pointed out that times had changed—Osama bin Laden,

African-American Senators

Carol Moseley Braun, also from Illinois, served in the U.S. Senate from 1993 to 1999. She was the last African-American U.S. senator prior to Barack Obama's election in 2004.

Only three African-Americans had previously been elected to the U.S. Senate. The first two were from Mississippi after the American Civil War. Hiram Rhodes Revels served from 1870 to 1871, and Blanche K. Bruce served from 1875 to 1881. Edward Brooke of Massachusetts served from 1967 to 1979.

Obama's race against Alan Keyes was the first time that two African Americans ran against each other for a seat in the U.S. Senate.

U.S. Government

The U.S. government has three branches. The president leads the executive branch, which is responsible for carrying out laws. The judicial branch, headed by the Supreme Court, decides if laws follow the U.S. Constitution. The legislative branch, or Congress, writes new laws for the country.

Congress is divided into the Senate and the House of Representatives. The Senate has 100 members, called senators. There are two senators from each state. Senators serve six-year terms. Every two years, approximately one-third of its seats are up for election. The House of Representatives has 435 members. Each state has a different number of representatives, based on its population. Every member of the House must face the voters every two years.

the leader of the terrorist group al-Qaeda, had come to dominate the front page of newspapers. Suddenly the name "Obama," sounding similar, might raise suspicion in a frightened nation. Altering the name, however, or using the nickname "Barry" from his younger days, could make people think that he had something to hide.

Obama was frustrated. He wondered where his political career was headed. As it turned out, Obama enjoyed his life for the next couple of years. He worked hard in the Illinois Senate. Free from planning the next move, he had a greater appreciation for his family—and his job.

ONE LAST SHOT

After reassessing his life and goals, Obama emerged with an idea. In 2003, he told Michelle he wanted to take one last shot. He would either move up in politics or get out altogether. He decided to make a run for U.S. Senate.

In the early stages of his run for a U.S. Senate seat, Obama tried to let people know who he was. As he detailed in *The Audacity of Hope*, Obama held press conferences to which no one came. He signed up for a St. Patrick's Day Parade and wound up in the last slot so that he and ten volunteers were marching just ahead of the sanitation workers cleaning up. They waved to the few people who were still watching as workers peeled decorative shamrocks off lampposts.

Obama wrote of the inefficient process,

> *Mostly though, I just traveled, often driving alone, first from ward to ward in Chicago, then from county to county and town to town, eventually up and down the state, past miles and miles of cornfields and beanfields and train tracks and silos.*[2]

Early on, the race looked tough. If he could win his party's primary, which was far from certain at that time, Obama would run against Republican Peter Fitzgerald. Fitzgerald had unseated Democrat Carol Moseley Braun in the previous election. Moseley Braun was considering another try and there were other significant Democratic hopefuls.

BREEZING TO VICTORY

Soon, however, the landscape began to change. Fitzgerald decided to leave the seat. Moseley Braun decided not to run. Obama won 52 percent of the vote in the 2004 Democratic primary. He beat multimillionaire businessman Blair Hull, Illinois Comptroller Daniel Hynes, and four others.

Even before Obama made his appearance at the 2004 Democratic National Convention, his Republican rival Jack Ryan was in trouble. Ryan was a former investment banker who had won the Republican primary. Scandals involving his former wife caused him to withdraw from the race in June. In the time before a new Republican nominee came forward, Obama had no one to run against. Meanwhile, he went to help John Kerry's presidential campaign. His work with Kerry allowed him to make his attention-grabbing speech.

The Republican Party brought in former presidential candidate Alan Keyes to run against Obama. Keyes, however, was unable to mount a serious threat. Obama rolled to the largest electoral victory in Illinois history, gaining 70 percent of the votes to 27 percent for Keyes.

Obama and other new senators are sworn in by
Vice President Dick Cheney, foreground.

Michelle Obama recognized the historical significance of her husband's election to the U.S. Senate.

We ignored the odds. We didn't vote for the richest candidate. We didn't vote for the best-connected candidate. We didn't vote for the slickest-talking candidate. What we did today was vote for the best candidate for the job.[3]

Dick Durbin, a fellow Democrat and the other U.S. senator from Illinois, said Obama's high profile put him in position to make an immediate impact. "Most people know him because he's a national figure with that wonderful speech at our convention," Durbin said. "Since that convention, he has helped so many senators."[4] Despite Obama's rookie status, he was able to become one of the nation's best-known and most influential senators.

How a Bill Becomes a Law

Any member of the U.S. House of Representatives or U.S. Senate can introduce a bill. Next, the leader of the Senate or House decides which committee looks at the bill. Bills are sometimes split among more than one committee. Sometimes, the committee has a time limit for how long they can review the bill.

The committee decides if the full House or Senate should vote on the bill. A bill is "killed" if the committee decides it will not go to a vote. The leader of the Senate or House decides when the vote will occur. There are many rules governing how the vote will be handled and how long the House or Senate will discuss the bill.

Once the bill has passed in one house of Congress, it must also pass in the other house. Sometimes, a "conference committee" will meet to write a version of the bill that both houses are willing to pass. The bill is sent to the president to sign or veto. If the president signs the bill, it becomes a law. If the president vetoes a bill, it can still become a law if two-thirds of Congress votes to override the veto.

Passing Laws

Obama took office on January 4, 2005. He soon cosponsored a bill with Oklahoma Republican Tom Coburn. The bill would require the Office of Management and Budget to create a Web site listing all the organizations that receive money from the government. Each organization would be listed by name, location, and the amount of money it received each year.

Obama said in a press release,

At the very least, taxpayers deserve to know where their money is being spent. This common-sense legislation would shine a bright light on all federal spending to help prevent tax dollars from being wasted. If government spending can't withstand public scrutiny, then the money shouldn't be spent.[5]

Less than two years into his first term as a U.S. senator, the bill passed. The Federal Funding Accountability and Transparency Act was a way to protect taxpayers and rebuild trust in the government. The bill allowed every American to go online and see how and where their tax dollars were spent. Obama and Coburn were present on September 26, 2006, when President George W. Bush signed the bill into law.

Original Plan

Thomas Jefferson, the third president of the United States, had a vision. "We might hope to see the finances of the Union as clear and intelligible as a merchant's books, so that every member of Congress and every man of any mind in the Union should be able to comprehend them, to investigate abuses, and consequently to control them," Jefferson said.[6]

Without the Internet and modern computers, what Jefferson hoped for in 1802 was not possible. More than 200 years later, the passage of the Federal Funding Accountability and Transparency Act in 2006 made Jefferson's dream a reality.

President Bush signed the Federal Funding Accountability and Transparency Act in 2006.

SENATOR IN ACTION

Tracing back to his days with the *Harvard Law Review*, Obama's work as a senator centered on the belief that people with different views could unite to solve problems. As a U.S. senator, he worked to stop corruption in Congress with his Federal Funding Accountability and Transparency Act. He also worked to represent veterans, reduce the nation's dependence on foreign oil, and address concerns about terrorism and national security.

In the U.S. Senate, Obama served on the Health, Education, Labor and Pensions Committee, the Foreign Relations Committee, and the Veterans Affairs Committee. During the first two years of his term in the U.S. Senate, Obama also served on the Environment and Public Works Committee.

On the Veterans Affairs Committee, Obama fought to help Illinois veterans receive the disability pay they were promised. He worked with the Veterans Administration to make plans to care for the thousands of veterans who would be returning from Iraq and Afghanistan.

Obama realized the threat posed by unsecured deadly weapons, which could potentially fall into the hands of terrorists. He traveled to Russia with Republican U.S. Senator Dick Lugar. Together, Obama and Lugar

The War in Iraq

After the terrorist attacks of September 11, 2001, President Bush said that the ruler of Iraq, Saddam Hussein, had dangerous weapons. Bush wanted to go to war against Hussein.

Obama was a state senator in Illinois when he spoke out against a possible war with Iraq. "I am not opposed to all wars," Obama said in 2002. "I'm opposed to dumb wars."[7]

Obama acknowledged Hussein was a "bad guy," but said that Hussein could be stopped without war. Obama thought that a war in Iraq would be difficult to end and many lives would be lost. He worried that war would make the Middle East less safe.

The conflict in Iraq began in 2003. By 2008, the war had cost billions of dollars and thousands of soldiers' lives.

worked on new efforts to find and secure deadly weapons around the world. Obama also tried to work with both parties and with auto companies, unions, farmers, and businesses to encourage more alternative fuels and higher fuel standards for cars. ⁓

Pictures of Dr. Martin Luther King Jr. and President Abraham Lincoln hung on the wall in Obama's senate office.

Obama officially announced his candidacy for president outside the Old State Capitol in Springfield, Illinois, on February 10, 2007.

PRESIDENTIAL CONTENDER

fter Obama's speech at the 2004 Democratic National Convention, people began to believe that he could be a presidential candidate in the next election. Even before Obama entered the race, he polled in second place among Democratic hopefuls. He was second to Hillary Clinton, the U.S. senator from New York and wife of former President Bill Clinton. On February 10, 2007, Obama stood before thousands in Springfield, Illinois, and declared that he would be a candidate for the Democratic presidential nomination.

Obama referenced another former Illinois politician, President Abraham Lincoln, in his announcement:

> *In the shadow of the Old State Capitol, where Lincoln once called on a divided house to stand together, where common hopes and common dreams still live, I stand before you today and announce my candidacy for president of the United States of America.* [1]

Two-way Race

Joe Biden, Chris Dodd, John Edwards, Mike Gravel, Dennis Kucinich, and Bill Richardson joined Obama and Clinton as candidates. However, the leading candidates were Obama and Clinton when the race started with the Iowa caucus on January 3, 2008. A month into the primary season, none of the other candidates remained active.

Obama won in Iowa, gaining 39 percent of the votes. Edwards came in second at 30 percent, just ahead of Clinton's 29 percent. Iowa was the only state in which any candidate other than Obama and Clinton finished in the top two. Obama and Clinton occupied the top spots—in either order—for the rest of the primary season.

Biden and Dodd left the race after finishing fifth and seventh out of eight in the Iowa caucus. Richardson dropped out after the next primary in New Hampshire. Gravel bowed out after finishing fourth in Michigan on January 15. Kucinich left the race days later and Edwards pulled out by the end of the month. Obama led throughout the primary season, but Clinton was seldom far behind.

Delegates are won in each state. The number of delegates per state depends on the population of that state. A candidate needed to win at least 2,118 delegates to become the Democratic Party's choice. By June 3, 2008, Obama had 2,201 delegates to Clinton's 1,896. That gave him enough votes to win the primary.

Family on Campaign

On the campaign trail, the Obama family had game nights and date nights whenever Obama was home for a couple of days. Michelle said that his job while he was campaigning was to be there for the most important things:

"Right now, it's important for him to be at parent-teacher conferences, piano recitals, things that are important to the girls . . . There are few things that he's missed that were important to them."[2]

Obama won a hard-fought democratic primary against Senator Hillary Clinton.

The Democratic Party would officially choose him as its nominee at the Democratic National Convention in Denver, Colorado, on August 27.

Obama became the first African American to win the nomination of a major political party. He was now closer to the presidency than any minority who had come before him.

FALL CAMPAIGN

The next step for Obama was to select his running mate, the vice presidential candidate for the 2008 general election. Obama chose Biden, a longtime U.S. senator from Delaware, on August 23.

Biden had dropped out early in his second attempt at obtaining the Democratic presidential nomination. His experience as a U.S. senator since 1973 seemed to work well in combination with Obama's youth. Biden was also widely respected for his foreign policy expertise.

After the Democratic National Convention on August 25–28, the campaign kicked into high gear. Obama, Biden, and other Democratic leaders began traveling across the country, speaking to huge rallies, television audiences, and groups of all sizes.

The week of September 1, 2008, the Republican Party

2008 Democratic Candidates

The candidates that Barack Obama ran against in the 2008 Democratic primaries were:

- Joe Biden, the six-term U.S. senator from Delaware who also ran for president in 1988
- Hillary Clinton, the former First Lady and current U.S. senator from New York
- Chris Dodd, a U.S. senator from Connecticut since 1981
- John Edwards, a former U.S. senator from North Carolina who was the Democratic vice-presidential nominee in 2004
- Mike Gravel, a former U.S. senator from Alaska
- Dennis Kucinich, a member of the U.S. House of Representatives from Ohio and a presidential candidate in the 2004 primary
- Bill Richardson, the governor of New Mexico and a former U.S. energy secretary, UN ambassador, and member of the U.S. House of Representatives

held its own convention. There, Obama's opponent, John McCain, announced his running mate. His choice, Alaska governor Sarah Palin, energized the Republican Party. After the excitement of the Republican National Convention, John McCain's poll numbers rose. For a short time, the Republican was leading.

However, Obama was able to pull ahead again. His message of hope and change resonated with the American people. His huge network of grassroots support improved his fund-raising and get-out-the-vote efforts. Millions of people around the country of all ages and all races were enthusiastic and excited about Obama's candidacy—because he would be the first African-American president, but also because they believed that he could make the United States a better place for everyone.

As Obama began his first term as president, he faced many challenges. The nation was fighting two wars, in Afghanistan and in Iraq, and faced other

New Technology

One reason for Obama's overwhelming success was his campaign's use of new technology. Internet groups, e-mails, and text messages organized his supporters and increased his fund-raising abilities.

Before taking the stage at Grant Park, Obama sent an e-mail to his supporters. "I'm about to head to Grant Park to talk to everyone gathered there, but I wanted to write to you first. We just made history. And I don't want you to forget how we did it. . . . All of this happened because of you," he wrote.[4]

national security challenges. In September 2008, several major financial firms were forced to merge or close. The economy was in crisis as mortgages were foreclosed and people lost their savings and jobs. Obama was elected partially because of the people's hope that he could help fix the economy. In addition, the new president faced the growing problems of environmental concerns and a troubled health care system.

In his acceptance speech, Obama acknowledged that there was a difficult road ahead. He told the American people that they might have to make sacrifices, and that they might not always agree with his decisions. However, he promised to always be honest about the problems facing the country. He declared,

> The road ahead will be long. Our climb will be steep. We may not get there in one year or even one term, but America—I have never been more hopeful than I am tonight that we will get there. I promise you—we as a people will get there.[3]

President-elect Barack Obama waved to the crowd in Chicago
after giving his acceptance speech on November 4, 2008.

TIMELINE

1961	1967	1971
On August 4, Barack Obama Jr. is born in Hawaii.	Obama's family moves to Indonesia.	Obama returns to Hawaii from Indonesia to live with his grandparents, Stan and Madelyn Dunham.

1983	1990	1991
Obama graduates from Columbia University with a degree in political science.	On February 6, Obama is selected president of the *Harvard Law Review*.	In May, Obama graduates from Harvard Law School.

1979

1979

1981

Obama graduates from Punahou School, a high school in Hawaii.

Obama enters Occidental College in Los Angeles.

Obama transfers to Columbia University in New York City.

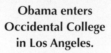

1992

1995

1996

On October 3, Obama marries Michelle Robinson in Chicago.

Obama's first book, *Dreams from My Father*, is released.

On November 5, Obama wins his first political race for the Illinois State Senate.

TIMELINE

1998	2000	2001
On July 4, Obama's daughter Malia is born.	Obama falls short in a run for the U.S. House of Representatives.	On June 7, Obama's daughter Sasha is born.

2006	2006	2007
On April 7, Tom Coburn and Obama cosponsor the Federal Funding Accountability and Transparency Act.	On September 26, President Bush signs the Federal Funding Accountability and Transparency Act into law.	On February 10, Obama announces that he will seek the Democratic nomination for the 2008 presidential race.

2004

On July 27, Obama delivers the keynote speech at the Democratic National Convention.

2004

Obama is elected to the U.S. Senate.

2006

Obama's book *The Audacity of Hope* is released.

2008

On June 3, Obama clinches the number of delegates required to be the Democrats' presidential nominee.

2008

On August 23, Obama announces that Joe Biden will be his vice presidential running mate in the election.

2008

On November 4, Obama is elected president of the United States.

ESSENTIAL FACTS

DATE OF BIRTH

August 4, 1961

PLACE OF BIRTH

Honolulu, Hawaii

PARENTS

Barack Obama Sr. and Stanley Ann (Dunham) Soetoro

EDUCATION

Punahou School, Honolulu, Hawaii; Occidental College, Los Angeles, California; Columbia University, New York City, New York; Harvard University Law School, Cambridge, Massachusetts

MARRIAGE

Michelle Robinson (October 3, 1992)

CHILDREN

Malia and Sasha

RESIDENCES

Honolulu, Hawaii; Jakarta, Indonesia; Los Angeles, California; New York City, New York; Cambridge, Massachusetts; Chicago, Illinois

CAREER HIGHLIGHTS

❖ First African-American president of the *Harvard Law Review*, 1990

❖ Taught law at the University of Chicago, 1992–2004

❖ Elected to the Illinois State Senate, 1996

❖ Keynote speaker at the Democratic National Convention, 2004

❖ Fifth African-American member of the U.S. Senate, 2004

❖ First African-American president of the United States, 2008

SOCIETAL CONTRIBUTION

As a community organizer, Obama registered voters on Chicago's South Side. As an Illinois state senator, he helped pass legislation to reform campaign finance and protect the rights of arrested people. As a U.S. senator, Obama cosponsored a bill that requires the government to list its spending online. He also has worked to help veterans, reduce the nation's reliance on foreign oil, and stop the international proliferation of deadly weapons.

CONFLICTS

Obama grew up without his father. He moved frequently as a child, and had trouble putting down roots. As a young man, Obama struggled to discover his identity as a biracial person. As an adult, Obama ran in several elections, including a 2000 loss for the U.S. House of Representatives.

QUOTE

"The road ahead will be long. Our climb will be steep. We may not get there in one year or even one term, but America—I have never been more hopeful than I am tonight that we will get there. I promise you—we as a people will get there."—*Barack Obama*

ADDITIONAL RESOURCES

SELECT BIBLIOGRAPHY

Obama, Barack. *The Audacity of Hope.* New York: Crown Publishing Group, 2006.

Obama, Barack. *Dreams from My Father: A Story of Race and Inheritance.* New York: Crown Publishing Group, 2007.

"The Online NewsHour: Vote 2008 The Primaries." *PBS.* 2008. <http://www.pbs.org/newshour/vote2008/primaries/candidates/obama.html>.

FURTHER READING

Obama, Barack, and Lisa Rogak. *Barack Obama in His Own Words.* New York: PublicAffairs, 2007.

Sapet, Kerrily. *Political Profiles: Barack Obama.* Greensboro, NC: Morgan Reynolds Publishing, 2007.

Thomas, Garen. *Yes We Can: A Biography of Barack Obama.* New York: Macmillan, 2008.

WEB LINKS

To learn more about Barack Obama, visit ABDO Publishing Company online at **www.abdopublishing.com**. Web sites about Barack Obama are featured on our Book Links page. These links are routinely monitored and updated to provide the most current information available.

Places to Visit

Illinois Old State Capitol
Old State Capitol Plaza, Springfield, IL 62701
217-785-7960
www.illinoishistory.gov/hs/old_capitol.htm
The Old State Capitol was the center of Illinois state government during the American Civil War and the site of several famous speeches by Abraham Lincoln. Obama announced his candidacy for U.S. president here in 2007.

United States Senate
United States Capitol Building, Washington, DC 20510
202-224-3121
www.senate.gov/visiting/common/generic/visiting_galleries.htm
The galleries of the U.S. Senate and the U.S. House of Representatives are open to view whenever either body is in session. Gallery passes, which can be obtained from the office of your senator or representative, are required to visit the galleries.

The White House
1600 Pennsylvania Ave NW, Washington, DC 20500
202-456-1414
www.whitehouse.gov/history/life/video/index.html
The White House is the home of the president and his or her family. It features the West Wing and the Oval Office, where the president and the president's staff work, as well as famous rooms such as the Blue Room and the Lincoln Bedroom. The White House allows tours by appointment.

GLOSSARY

apartheid
> A political policy of racial segregation.

asbestos
> Fireproof insulating materials whose fibers have been linked to cancer.

biracial
> A person who has parents from two racial groups.

campaign
> A series of events planned to help a candidate win an election.

candidate
> Someone who runs for political office.

caucus
> A meeting of a group of persons belonging to a political party in order to select a candidate.

communism
> A political system in which the government owns all the property.

comptroller
> A public official who monitors government accounts and spending.

convention
> An assembly of people for a common purpose, such as the nomination of a political candidate.

delegate
> A representative to a convention who selects a candidate on behalf of the voters.

Electoral College
> The group of electors that casts each states' votes for president and vice president.

government
> The organization through which a political unit exercises authority.

inauguration
  A ceremony of induction into political office.

keynote speech
  An address designed to present the primary interest of an assembly, such as a political party, while increasing unity and enthusiasm.

nomination
  The act or process of choosing a candidate for office.

president
  The top elected official in the U.S. government.

primary
  A beginning step in the election process in which a party chooses its candidate for an office.

scholarship
  An award of money to assist with educational expenses.

teleprompter
  A device used to unroll a magnified script in front of someone who is speaking.

veto
  The power to refuse approval.

vice president
  The person second in command to the president who serves in the president's absence or disability.

SOURCE NOTES

Chapter 1. The New President
1. "Full Transcript: Sen. Barack Obama's Victory Speech." *abcnews. com*. 4 Nov. 2008. 5 Nov. 2008 <http://abcnews.go.com/Politics/Vote2008/story?id=6181477&page=1>.
2. Ibid.
3. "African-Americans Savor a Historic Moment." *msnbc.com*. 5 Nov. 2008. 5 Nov. 2008 <http://www.msnbc.msn.com/id/27547171/>.
4. "Transcript of Obama's Speech." *cnn.com* <http://cnn.com>. 18 March 2008. 5 Nov. 2008 <http://www.cnn.com/2008/POLITICS/03/18/obama.transcript/>.

Chapter 2. A Boy Named Barry
1. Barack Obama. *Dreams from My Father*. New York: Crown Publishing Group, 2004. 36.
2. Kirsten Scharnberg and Kim Barker. "The not-so-simple story of Barack Obama's youth." *Chicago Tribune*. 25 Mar. 2007. 21 Sept. 2008 <http://www.chicagotribune.com/news/politics/obama/chi-070325obama-youth-story-archive,0,3864722.story>.

Chapter 3. College and Community
1. Larry Gordon. "Occidental recalls 'Barry' Obama." *Los Angeles Times*. 29 Jan. 2007. 22 Sept. 2008 < http://articles.latimes.com/2007/jan/29/local/me-oxy29>.
2. Ibid.
3. Ibid.
4. Barack Obama. *Dreams from My Father*. New York: Crown Publishing Group, 2004. 115.
5. Ibid. 115–116.
6. Shira Boss-Bicak. "Barack Obama '83: Is He the New Face of The Democratic Party?" *Columbia College Today*. Jan. 2005. 23 Sept. 2008 <http://www.college.columbia.edu/cct_archive/jan05/cover.php>.
7. Ibid.
8. Barack Obama. *Dreams from My Father*. New York: Crown Publishing Group, 2004. 188.
9. Kenneth T. Walsh. "On the Streets of Chicago, a Candidate Comes of Age." *U.S. News and World Reports*. 26 Aug. 2007.

23 Sept. 2008 <http://www.usnews.com/usnews/news/
articles/070826/30bama.htm>

10. Ibid.

11. Ryan Lizza. "The Agitator." *The New Republic.* 19 Mar. 2007. 2
Oct. 2008 <http://www.tnr.com/story_print.html?id=a74fca23-
f6ac-4736-9c78-f4163d4f25c7>.

Chapter 4. The Lawyer

1. Barack Obama. *Dreams from My Father.* New York: Crown Publishing
Group, 2004. 220.

2. Ibid.

3. Tammerlin Drummond. "Barack Obama's Law Personality."
Los Angeles Times. 19 Mar. 1990. 3 Oct. 2008 <http://latimesblogs.
latimes.com/thedailymirror/2008/09/barack-obama-ha.html>.

4. Michael Levenson and Jonathan Saltzman. "At Harvard Law, a
Unifying Voice." *Boston Globe.* 28 Jan. 2007. 2 Aug. 2008 <http://
www.boston.com/news/local/articles/2007/01/28/at_harvard_law_a_
unifying_voice/>.

5. Ibid.

6. Shira Boss-Bicak. "Barack Obama '83: Is He the New Face of
The Democratic Party?" *Columbia College Today.* Jan. 2005. Sept. 23
2008 <http://www.college.columbia.edu/cct_archive/jan05/cover.
php>.

7. Abdon M. Pallasch. "Law students gave Obama big thumbs-
up." *Chicago Sun Times.* 18 Dec. 2007. 23 Sept. 2008 <http://
www.suntimes.com/news/politics/obama/701490,CST-NWS-
obamaprof18.article>.

Chapter 5. Entering Politics

1. Kenneth T. Walsh. "Obama's Years in Chicago Politics Shaped
His Presidential Candidacy." *U.S. News and World Report.* 11 Apr.
2008. 2 Oct. 2008 <http://www.usnews.com/articles/news/
campaign-2008/2008/04/11/obamas-years-in-chicago-politics-
shaped-his-presidential-candidacy.html>.

2. David Jackson and Ray Long. "Barack Obama: Showing his
bare knuckles." *Chicago Tribune.* 4 Apr. 2007. 24 Sept. 2008
<http://www.chicagotribune.com/news/politics/obama/chi-
070403088iapr04-archive,0,5507395.story>.

SOURCE NOTES CONTINUED

3. Ibid.

4. Ibid.

5. Janny Scott. "In 2000, a Streetwise Veteran Schooled a Bold Young Obama." *New York Times*. 9 Sept. 2007. 30 Sept. 2008 <http://www.nytimes.com/2007/09/09/us/politics/09obama.html>.

6. Janny Scott. "In Illinois, Obama Proved Pragmatic and Shrewd." *New York Times*. 30 July 2007. 30 Sept. 2008 <http://www.nytimes.com/2007/07/30/us/politics/30obama.html>.

Chapter 6. Family Life

1. "Obama: Daughters not impressed by candidacy." *msnbc.com*. 29 Apr. 2008. 24 Sept. 2008 <http://www.msnbc.msn.com/id/24370175/>.

2. Ibid.

3. "Meet the Obamas." *barackobama.com*. 24 Sept. 2008 <http://www.barackobama.com/learn/meet_michelle.php>.

4. Barack Obama. *The Audacity of Hope*. New York: Crown Publishing Group, 2006. 342.

5. Stephen M. Silverman. "Barack Obama's 9-year-old Shuns Hiltons." *People*. 1 Oct. 2007. 20 Oct. 2008. <http://www.people.com/people/article/0,,20091040,00.html>.

Chapter 7. The Speech

1. Eli Saslow. "The 17 Minutes That Launched a Political Star." *Washington Post*. 25 Aug. 2008. 24 Sept. 2008 <http://www.washingtonpost.com/wp-dyn/content/article/2008/08/24/AR2008082401671_2.html?nav=hcmodule>.

2. Ibid.

3. Ibid.

4. "Transcript: Illinois Senate Candidate Barack Obama." *Washington Post*. 27 July 2004. 25 Aug. 2008 <http://www.washingtonpost.com/wp-dyn/articles/A19751-2004Jul27.html>.

5. Eli Saslow. "The 17 Minutes That Launched a Political Star." *Washington Post*. 25 Aug. 2008. 24 Sept. 2008 <http://www.washingtonpost.com/wp-dyn/content/article/2008/08/24/AR2008082401671_2.html?nav=hcmodule>.

6. Ibid.

Chapter 8. National Office

1. Barack Obama. *The Audacity of Hope.* New York: Crown Publishing Group, 2006. 3.

2. Ibid. 6.

3. Caroline Kim. "Election: Obama becomes fifth black senator in nation's history." *Daily Illini.* 3 Nov. 2004. 4 Aug. 2008 <http://media.www.dailyillini.com/media/storage/paper736/news/2004/11/03/News/Election.Obama.Becomes.Fifth.Black.Senator.In.Nations.History-791195.shtml>.

4. Ibid.

5. "Obama, Coburn Introduce Bill Requiring Public Disclosure of All Recipients of Federal Funding." *Senate Press Release.* 7 Apr. 2006. 25 Sept. 2008 <http://obama.senate.gov/press/060407-coburn_introduc/>.

6. Albert Ellery Bergh, ed. *The Writings of Thomas Jefferson.* Volume 9. Washington DC: Thomas Jefferson Memorial Association, 1907. 307. Original from Harvard University. Digitized 31 July 2006. 23 October 2008 <http://books.google.com/books?id=3_GHSPlgmdgC&printsec=titlepage&client=firefox-a#PRA3-PA307,M1>.

7. "Barack Obama." *biography.com.* 26 Sept. 2008 <http://www.biography.com/featured-biography/barack-obama/index.jsp>.

Chapter 9. Presidential Contender

1. "Obama declares he's running for president." *cnn.com.* 10 Feb. 2007. 26 Sept. 2008 <http://www.cnn.com/2007/POLITICS/02/10/obama.president/index.html>.

2. Sandra Sobieraj Westfall. "Barack Obama Gives Daughter $1 Allowance a Week." *People.* 28 July 2008. 8 Oct. 2008 <http://www.people.com/people/article/0,,20214569_3,00.html>.

3. "Full Transcript: Sen. Barack Obama's Victory Speech." *abcnews.com.* 4 Nov. 2008. 5 Nov. 2008 <http://abcnews.go.com/Politics/Vote2008/story?id=6181477&page=1>.

4. "Message from Barack Obama: How this happened." *my.barackobama.com.* 5 Nov. 2008. 6 Nov. 2008 <http://my.barackobama.com/page/community/post/stateupdates/gGx3GM>.

INDEX

ABOUT THE AUTHOR

Tom Robinson is a freelance writer and editor of educational
material. He has written 15 nonfiction books, most of which
were created for young readers. A former newspaper reporter
and editor, Robinson was honored by the Associated Press Sports
Editors for one of the top ten news stories in the nation in 1998 for
newspapers in the 50,000–140,000 circulation category. He lives
in Pennsylvania with his family.

PHOTO CREDITS